ON MAN!

WANTED!

WANTED!

ONAL
NAL!

WANTED!

For Steven Malk

VIKING
Published by the Penguin Group
Penguin Group (USA) LLC
375 Hudson Street
New York, New York 10014

USA * Canada * UK * Ireland * Australia
New Zealand * India * South Africa * China

penguin.com
A Penguin Random House Company

First published in the United States of America by Viking,
an imprint of Penguin Young Readers Group, 2015

LIBRARY OF CONGRESS CATALOGING-IN-PUBLICATION DATA IS AVAILABLE
ISBN: 978-0-670-01652-5

Manufactured in China

10   9   8   7   6   5   4   3   2   1

Designed by Greg Pizzoli and Jim Hoover   Set in Sentinel Book

The Impossibly True Story of

TRICKY VIC

the Man Who Sold the Eiffel Tower

GREG PIZZOLI

VIKING

An Imprint of Penguin Group (USA)

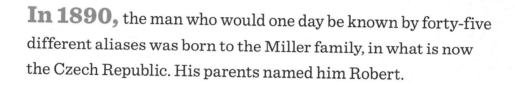

In 1890, the man who would one day be known by forty-five different aliases was born to the Miller family, in what is now the Czech Republic. His parents named him Robert.

AS A YOUNG MAN, Robert Miller was a gifted student with a seemingly bright future ahead of him.

Report to Parents of
Scholar's Attendance, Conduct, and Progress
FOR THE TERM ENDED *June 22, 1903*

Name *Robert Miller*

Arithmetic ... V.G.	Literature ... G.	Appearance ... Ex.
Reading ... G.	History ... G.	Theater ... Ex.
Writing ... G.	Geography ... V.G.	Conduct ... F.

K.W. *Head Teacher*

J Hoover *Class Teacher*

NOTE:
Ex. = Excellent;
V.G. = Very Good;
G. = Good;
F. = Fair.

He was fluent in several languages, and his father urged him to study hard and complete a degree at the University of Paris. But, before finishing his studies, and against his parents' wishes, he left home to become "an artist."

A CON ARTIST!

Ah, yes.
But an *artist*
all the same.

2

AFTER LEAVING SCHOOL, he began playing poker and billiards, and found he was quite skilled at both. He frequented bars and gambling houses, earning his living as a professional gambler.

Miller ran into his first bit of trouble at the age of nineteen, when he began to flirt with the wife of a man whom he was beating at poker. The man became enraged and cut Miller's face with a knife, leaving Miller with a distinctive scar that went from his left ear down to his jaw.

EAGER TO LEAVE this trouble behind him, Miller took his gambling talents to the seas, trying his skills aboard transatlantic ocean liners. He created the alias of "Count Victor Lustig" so he would fit in with the aristocrats and millionaires who took steamships from Paris to New York. He would chat up wealthy passengers and, over the course of the trip, gain their trust. The voyage took about a week, just enough time for a con artist with his talents to befriend his fellow travelers and invite them to play a friendly game of cards.

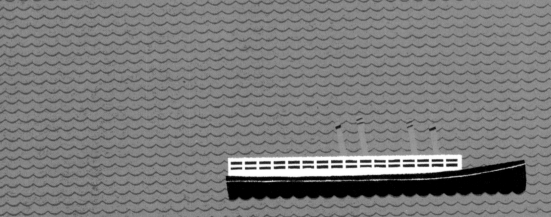

"Victor" was a convincing count: exceedingly well dressed, soft spoken, and always with lots of money to spare at the game tables. Once the ship docked and the passengers disembarked, "Count Lustig" would disappear, along with their money.

He robbed
my room!

He broke
my heart!

He drank
my gin!

The First World War put an end to the transatlantic ocean liner trips—and with them, Count Lustig's preferred lifestyle. He gambled around Europe for several years, but after wearing out his welcome in many major cities and being arrested several times, Vic decided to try his luck in the United States.

PROHIBITION

Prohibition was an effort to stop the American public's overconsumption of alcohol and to curb the drunken behavior that was seen as harmful to families and society as a whole. Protest groups such as the Anti-Saloon League convinced lawmakers that making or selling alcohol should be outlawed in the United States, and in 1920, with the passing of the Eighteenth Amendment, the United States government banned the sale, production, and transportation of all alcoholic products. However the new laws couldn't stop the flow of liquor. Vast criminal networks schemed to satisfy the public's thirst, turning crime lords such as Al Capone into national celebrities. Police and lawmakers were unable to keep the booze out of illegal bars known as "speakeasies" and "blind tigers," which were run by "bootleggers." Prohibition lasted until 1933, when it was repealed by the Twenty-First Amendment.

IN THE USA, crime was thriving. Prohibition was in full swing, and with the new laws came new crimes. Networks of bootleggers, speakeasies, and illegal gambling houses made certain there was always dishonest work available to those who wanted it.

Maybe we should scram?

Hic!

TOTALLY LEGIT

The most notorious of all criminals was Chicago mobster Al "Scarface" Capone. Any criminal who wanted to work in Chicago had to check in with Scarface first, and Tricky Vic was no exception.

The story goes that Victor—as he was now known to everyone except his family—went to see Capone while living in Chicago. He told Scarface he had a foolproof way to make a lot of money and just needed to borrow $50,000 to make it happen. Vic promised to double Capone's cash within one month's time.

At the end of the month, he went back to Capone and told him his plan had failed. The Chicago crime boss was furious—how dare this man think he could con the great Capone! But just as Scarface was about to explode . . . Victor handed him back his money. He apologized that he wasn't able to double it, but he returned it all.

Capone was so impressed with his honesty that he gave him $5,000 and his blessing to work within the Windy City.

And so Tricky Vic conned Capone. It seems returning the cash had been his plan all along; there never was a scheme to double the money. Victor borrowed it from Capone and placed it in a security lock box until the end of the month, simply so he could return it and gain the Big Boss's trust.

Once he had Capone's blessing, Tricky Vic was free to con his way across America, but he needed a plan. And it had to be good. Vic knew he couldn't work small cons forever—he needed a big score, something that would pull in a lot of money all at once.

During his steamship days, he had heard of a scam known as the Romanian Money Box, and he decided to try it out for himself.

The con went something like this:

"Count Victor Lustig" would hang around speakeasies and expensive hotels, arriving by limousine and always displaying an air of great sophistication.

NO VACANCY

Eventually, he would notice a well-to-do gentleman and casually start a conversation, learning as much as he could about the man's finances and assessing whether this "mark"—the planned victim of his scheme—was wealthy enough to be worth his time and trouble.

After gaining the confidence of his mark, he'd quietly mourn his own misfortunes, claiming that he was a count in name only—his family fortune had been stolen during the First World War. When pressed as to how he could afford limousines, fashionable clothes, and expensive hotels, Vic would "reluctantly" reveal the secret of his money-printing box.

Count Lustig would then invite the mark up to his room and bring out the impressive box. He'd carefully insert a single hundred-dollar bill into a slot at one end of the machine. Then, as he turned a few knobs, he would lament that the box's only flaw was that it took six hours to produce each bill.

This could take a while. Can I offer you another drink?

Thank you. That would be lovely.

He would buy the mark dinner and a few drinks, and after the required time had passed, out would pop a perfect copy of the hundred-dollar bill.

The mark, amazed at the device, would offer to buy it immediately. At first, Lustig would refuse, only making the buyer more desperate to have it, and driving up the price he was willing to pay. Finally, Lustig would agree to sell his machine.

In reality, the machine did no printing at all. It simply ejected bills that Lustig himself had already placed inside. He handed over the machine with just two hundred-dollar bills inside, which each took the necessary six hours to "print."

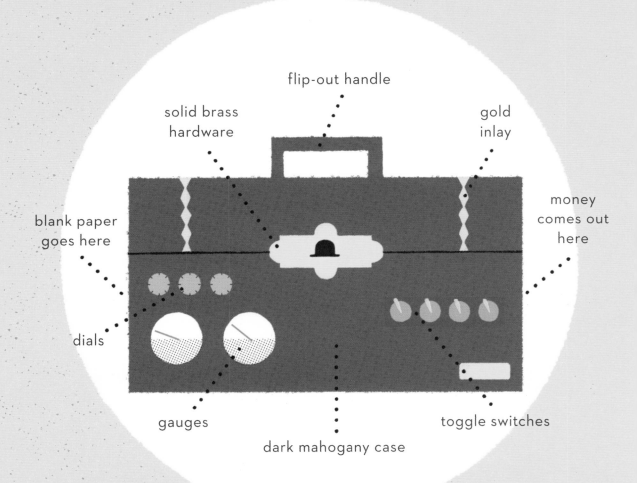

flip-out handle

solid brass hardware

gold inlay

blank paper goes here

money comes out here

dials

gauges

dark mahogany case

toggle switches

THE ROMANIAN MONEY BOX

After buying it from Lustig for tens of thousands of dollars, the new owner of the money box would run off to create his own falsely printed fortune. In time, the machine would slowly expose two more bills, but then it would shoot out only blank paper.

By the time the mark realized he had been scammed, Lustig was at least twelve hours away.

After a while, the police in the United States began to catch on to his tricks, and Vic knew he needed a change of scenery. He decided to flee the country and headed to Europe.

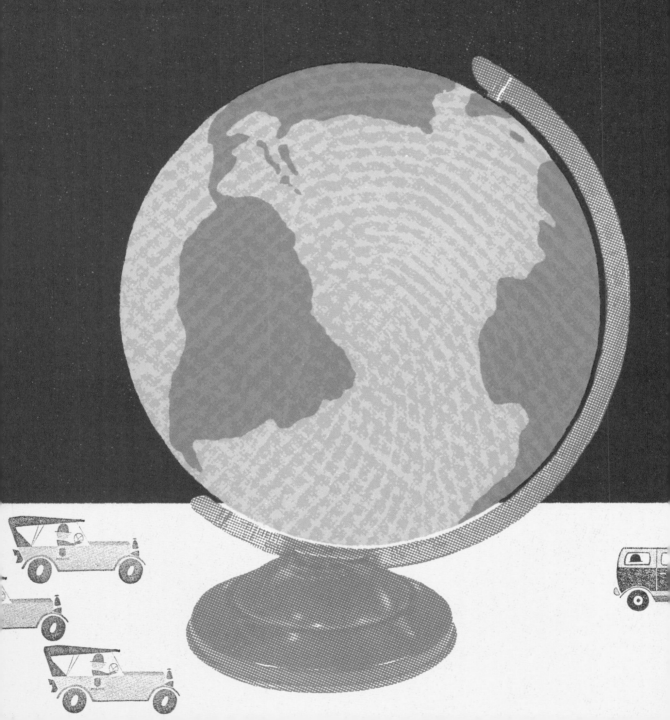

BACK ON HIS HOME TURF, Tricky Vic eventually settled in Paris, the City of Light, which seemed the perfect backdrop for "Count Victor Lustig" to stage his most spectacular scheme. Again he told himself he needed to pull off something big, a con that would secure his future for years to come.

Living in luxurious hotels under his alias, Victor spent his mornings in the park, reading the newspaper.

One day an article appeared that highlighted the many issues the city of Paris was having with the dilapidated Eiffel Tower. It was quickly falling into disrepair, and even basic upkeep was costing the city a fortune.

This gave Lustig an idea.

THE TOWER'S CRITICS

When it was first built in 1889, the Eiffel Tower had many critics. Newspapers published letters signed by prominent artists from the city who described Gustave Eiffel's design as "a truly tragic street-lamp" and an "iron gymnasium apparatus, incomplete, confused and deformed." When it was built, it was the tallest man-made structure in the world, and many thought it was unsafe, with some fearing that the tower would attract lightning storms to the area or be toppled by wind and fall onto nearby buildings.

The Count wasted no time. The next day he went to see a friend who ran a print shop to have phony business cards and stationery created. He gave himself the title "Deputy Director General of the Ministry of Posts and Telegraphs."

These look amazing!

Super.

He then called five of the most successful scrap metal dealers in Paris and set his plan in motion. He told them very little, saying only that he had a business proposition for them to consider, and that it was too delicate a matter to discuss on the telephone. For security purposes, it would be best to meet in person.

He invited the five men to the lavish Hôtel de Crillon, and after swearing them all to secrecy, Lustig revealed his secret.

The Eiffel Tower will be torn down, and one of you will be the man to do it.

Of course today this seems like a ridiculous proposition, but at the time it was not so far-fetched. The Eiffel Tower was built in 1889 as part of the Exposition Universelle, a world's fair coinciding with the one-hundred-year anniversary of the French Revolution. The great monument originally had been scheduled to be removed after twenty years, but that hadn't happened.

HÔTEL DE CRILLON

Though not as well known as the Eiffel Tower, the Hôtel de Crillon is a landmark in its own right. Located in central Paris, it was built in 1758 by King Louis XV as one of a pair of matching palaces. During the French Revolution, King Louis XVI was beheaded by guillotine directly in front of the building. The hotel opened to the public in 1909 and was a favorite of the world's politicians and celebrities, known for its spectacular views, delicious restaurant, and upscale patrons.

Lustig rented a limousine and took the scrap metal dealers on an "inspection tour" so that they could assess the site themselves and determine how much they would be willing to pay the government for the rights to dismantle the Eiffel Tower. The tower, over 1,000 feet tall, was constructed of 7,300 metric tons of iron, and 2.5 million rivets held it together, so whoever got the job would make a fortune from the sale of the scrap metal.

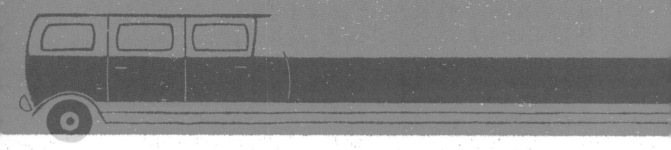

But first they would need to convince Count Victor Lustig that they could do it for the best price. Lustig asked them to propose how much they would pay for the rights, and to submit those "bids" to him at his hotel.

He urged them to move quickly, saying he needed the bids the next morning, and reminded them the plan must be kept secret. He warned that the news might cause a public outcry, and the government was doing everything it could to avoid a scandal.

The next morning, Tricky Vic, along with his assistant, "Dapper Don" Collins, awaited the bids from all five businessmen, although Vic knew all along who would get the job. His chosen mark was André Poisson, a relative newcomer to Paris, who was looking to make a name for himself in the elite Parisian society.

Poisson was thrilled at the prospect of taking on such a high-profile job and enthusiastically submitted a bid, which, of course, was accepted by Lustig.

He took the bait.

What a sap!

OPEN IN PRIVATE

They met again that afternoon to celebrate their shared
success. Poisson gave Lustig the cash, and Lustig supplied him
with all of the "official" paperwork.

After a few failed attempts to claim possession of the Eiffel Tower,
Poisson realized that he had been swindled, and yet, he did nothing.
He was humiliated and never contacted the police.

Someone with his insecurities about his social status would have
had trouble admitting that he had been duped at a game of cards,
let alone that he had lost his life savings to the "Deputy Director
General of the Ministry of Posts and Telegraphs," and it seems he
forfeited his fortune to save his reputation.

As for Tricky Victor Lustig, he and Collins (whose real name was Robert Tourbillon) made off to Vienna and waited for the story of the scam to break. When they saw no hint of the crime in French newspapers, they went back to Paris and tried the same con again.

This time, however, the mark went to the police, and Lustig was forced to make a quick getaway.

COUNTERFEITING

One of the oldest crimes known to man, counterfeiting is the creation of an imitation product, meant to trick others into thinking it is real.

Tricky Vic's success at counterfeiting US dollars with William Watts was simple; they made their counterfeit bills look perfectly genuine. They used high-quality paper and inks, and Watts was a master engraver, capable of producing extraordinary fakes.

Watts created metal plates drawn to exactly replicate each side of a $10 or $20 bill and then pressed the paper between two plates, creating perfect copies of US dollars.

FOR A TIME, Vic returned to his old money box scheme, and eventually he began to work as a professional counterfeiter. Assisted by several accomplices, including master counterfeiter William Watts, Tricky Vic flooded the United States with over one million dollars of forged cash.

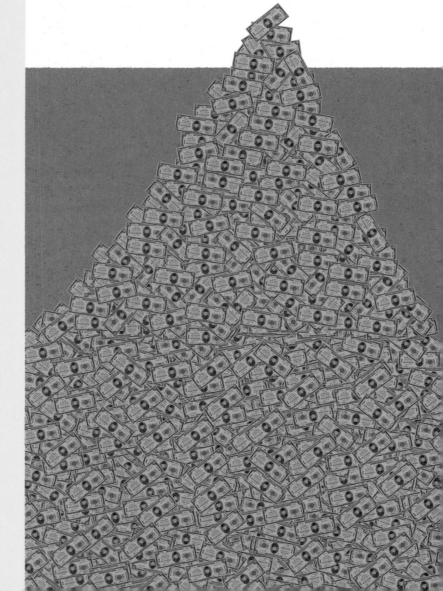

Tracking the phony dollars, police caught up with Watts, and quickly realized that "Count Victor" was involved. Two Secret Service agents arrested Tricky Vic in New York City in 1935.

He had two suitcases filled with clothes with him, but no fake currency, and no evidence on his person that pointed to counterfeiting, nothing unusual at all, except a small key.

Vic refused to say what the key was for—even suggesting that the agents had planted it on him during questioning. Eventually they discovered that the key opened a locker at a subway station in Times Square, and there they found plates for engraving fake bills and over $50,000 in counterfeit money.

Tricky Vic was charged and sent to the Federal House of Detention in New York City to await trial.

What's this?

What's what?

But the day before his scheduled trial in New York, Vic played one last con and escaped from prison by posing as a window washer.

In an amazing act of ingenuity, he tied together bed sheets and used them as a rope to climb from a third-floor prison window down to the ground below.

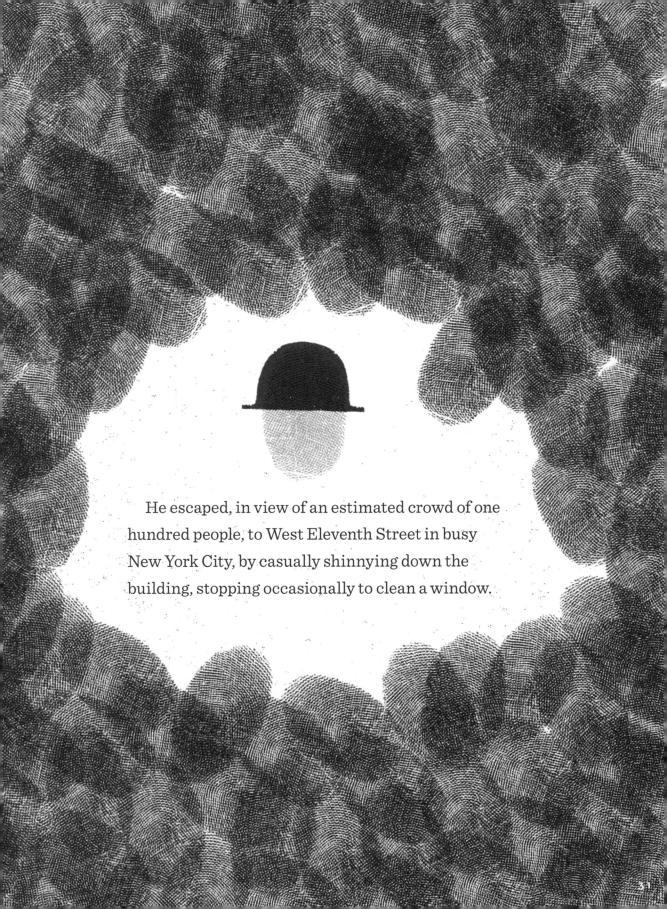

He escaped, in view of an estimated crowd of one hundred people, to West Eleventh Street in busy New York City, by casually shinnying down the building, stopping occasionally to clean a window.

WEST VALLEY INQUIRER
PHONY COUNT FLEES

DAILY EMPIRE NEWS
CROOKED COUNT LOOS

NEWS OF THE WORLD
TRICKSTER ON THE RUN!

THE BARNETT BUGLE
COUNTERFEIT COUNT

The newspapers covered the escape widely,
and Vic was recaptured a month later in Pittsburgh
after being recognized by his scar.

The police even brought in Dapper Don Collins, and a judge ordered Collins to testify against his old accomplice in the counterfeiting case.

ALCATRAZ

A former military prison, Alcatraz, often referred to by its nickname, "The Rock," is on an island located in the San Francisco Bay off the coast of California. From 1934 to 1963 it operated as a federal prison, holding prisoners deemed too difficult for other institutions.

Over the course of almost thirty years, a total of thirty-six inmates attempted to escape the island prison, but none is thought to have survived.

Today, the long-closed island prison is a National Historic Landmark and is open to tourists.

I ain't a rat.

Tricky Vic eventually pleaded guilty at trial and was sentenced to twenty years at the now legendary Alcatraz prison.

After serving twelve years in Alcatraz, Vic became
seriously ill and was transported to the Medical Center
for Federal Prisoners in Springfield, Missouri.

He died of pneumonia while there in 1947.

His death certificate printed only one name, Robert Miller, and his occupation was listed as "apprentice salesman."

The End

Glossary

Accomplice: a person who helps commit a crime

Alias: a name someone uses instead of their real name

Bid: to make an offer of a specific amount of money for an object or a job

Bootlegger: someone who illegally makes, transports, or sells alcohol

Con: the act of tricking another person by first gaining their confidence and trust

Con Artist: the person who performs the con on the mark

Count: a noble person of a European nation, usually from a wealthy family

Counterfeit: an imitation created to deceive others into thinking it is a genuine article (e.g., money, art, clothing)

Currency: the money (coins and bills) used by a specific country

Forgery: the act of counterfeiting (creating fake versions of) documents, signatures, or other genuine works

Mark: the victim of a con artist

Prohibition: the law forbidding the manufacture, transportation, and sale of alcohol within the United States, enacted by the Eighteenth Amendment to the Constitution

Scam: a trick or swindle performed by a confidence artist on a victim or "mark"

Scrap Metal: discarded metal to be sold for reuse (i.e., melted down and repurposed)

Speakeasy: a bar that sells alcoholic drinks illegally, also known as a "blind tiger" or "blind pig"

Selected Sources

Sincere thanks to the authors of the following books, newspaper articles, and websites, which were very helpful while writing and illustrating this book.

Books

Blundell, Nigel. *The Sting: True Stories of the World's Greatest Conmen.* London: John Blake, 2004.

Cook, Roger, and Tim Tate. *Roger Cook's Ten Greatest Conmen.* London: John Blake, 2008.

Johnson, James Francis, and Floyd Miller. *The Man Who Sold the Eiffel Tower.* Garden City, N.Y.: Doubleday, 1961.

Jonnes, Jill. *Eiffel's Tower: The Thrilling Story behind Paris's Beloved Monument and the Extraordinary World's Fair That Introduced It.* New York: Penguin, 2009.

Lindskoog, Kathryn. *Fakes, Frauds & Other Malarky: 301 Amazing Stories and How Not to be Fooled.* Grand Rapids, Mich.: Zondervan Publishing House, 1993.

Maurer, David W. *The Big Con: The Story of the Confidence Man.* New York: Anchor, 1999.

Morton, James, and Hilary Bateson. *Conned: Scams, Frauds and Swindles.* London: Piatkus, 2007.

Sifakis, Carl. *Hoaxes and Scams: A Compendium of Deceptions, Ruses, and Swindles.* New York: Facts on File, 1993.

Newspaper Articles

"Fight Extradition on Charge of Fraud: Missourian Accused of Getting $10,000 from Bank by Switching Envelopes." *The New York Times,* 28 May 1922.

"Parisian Sleuths Nab Scarface's Slick Henchmen." *Chicago Daily Tribune,* 6 July 1929.

"Count Seized Here with Bogus $51,000." *The New York Times,* 14 May 1935.

"Federal Men Arrest Count, Get Fake Cash." *Chicago Daily Tribune,* 14 May 1935.

"Robert Miller, Swindler, Flees Federal Prison." *Chicago Daily Tribune,* 2 Sept. 1935.

"The Count Escapes Jail on Sheet Rope." *The New York Times,* 2 Sept. 1935.

"Dapper Don Freed, but Gets Subpoena." *The New York Times,* 4 Sept. 1935.

"$1,000,000 Bogus Bill Ring Smashed by Raid in Jersey." *The New York Times,* 20 Sept. 1935.

"Collins Must Give Aid in Lustig Case." *The New York Times,* 21 Sept. 1935.

"Fugitive Count First to Face New Penalty." *The New York Times,* 24 Sept. 1935.

"Count Lustig Is Seized in Pittsburgh." *The New York Times,* 29 Sept. 1935.

"Lustig Back, Gets a Cell in Tombs." *The New York Times,* 1 Oct. 1935.

"Count Lustig Reveals Escape Technique, but Conceals How He Got Wire Nippers." *The New York Times,* 2 Oct. 1935.

"Counterfeiting Count Lustig Pleads Guilty." *Chicago Daily Tribune,* 6 Dec. 1935.

"Lustig Pleads Guilty as a Counterfeiter." *The New York Times,* 6 Dec. 1935.

"Lustig Sentenced to Twenty-Year Term." *The New York Times,* 10 Dec. 1935.

Websites

www.biography.com/people/victor-lustig-20657385

www.uselessinformation.org/lustig

www.smithsonianmag.com/history/the-smoothest-con-man-that-ever-lived-29861908

www.radio.cz/en/section/czechs/victor-lustig-the-man-who-could-have-sold-the-world

Author's Note

WHILE RESEARCHING this book, the same question kept coming up in my mind: *How can this be true?* It's all so incredible. And much of what I *think* is true about Robert Miller comes from other books, newspapers, and websites, which regularly contradict one another. In the many tellings of his life that I've found, the names, places, and sequence of events are often confused, so it's hard to trust any single source as being 100 percent accurate. Robert Miller was a con artist, after all! He was adept at disguising reality and creating his own truth. As the author, I did a little of that myself. For example, most accounts suggest that Vic conned Capone *after* the sale of the Eiffel Tower, not before. I wrote it in the order I did because I think the development of Vic's character in the narrative arc of the book takes precedence. I'm clarifying it here because I wouldn't want you to feel as though you've been conned. And while newspaper accounts of "Count Lustig" escaping from prison, operating a counterfeit ring, and selling the Romanian Money Box were easy enough to find, the hard facts about the sale of the Eiffel Tower remain elusive. But I think that's to be expected. After all, the truth, especially about a man who spent his life masquerading behind fake identities, can be tricky.

Paris still has con artists today, as I learned when I traveled there a few years ago. The courtyard of Musée de l'Orangerie is a nice spot to enjoy a packed lunch, and my wife and I were walking to a bench when a man a few yards ahead of us stopped suddenly and picked up something off the ground. He looked around quizzically and then asked us if we had dropped anything. He was holding a simple gold ring, like a wedding band. We hadn't dropped it, so we said, "No, but thanks," and hurried off, eager to eat our lunch.

September 1935: Robert Miller, aka Victor Lustig (right), on his way to Alcatraz prison.

As we ate, we noticed that a woman nearby was approaching another couple and asking them if they had dropped something: a small, glittering, gold ring. This was their con. They purposefully dropped a fake gold ring on the ground and then pretended to find it, asking if it belonged to tourists walking by this very popular museum. The tourists would consider the ring, a conversation would start, and always the con would ask the mark if they wanted to buy the ring. "Only ten Euros, if you'd like to keep it for yourself." As we ate our lunch, we saw this scenario play out a half dozen times. Theirs was a small and simple game, but even so, I was fascinated as I watched these tricksters work their con. And although their scheme lacked the smooth sophistication and imagination that attracted me to the stories of Victor Lustig, it was apparent to me then that the world of cons, scams, and marks is still thriving in the shadow of the Eiffel Tower today. Stay sharp.

ACKNOWLEDGMENTS

I'd like to first thank my editors, Ken Wright and Leila Sales, for their guidance, my art director, Jim Hoover, for his vision, and my literary agent, Steven Malk, for his passionate support of my work. Sincere thanks also to my friends Mac Barnett, Brian Biggs, Tim Gough, Rotem Moscovich, Zach OHora, Matt Phelan, Bob Shea, Lori Spencer, Sally and Laurent Gerome, my family, and especially, my wife, Kay.

This book would not exist if not for their combined efforts.

A NOTE ABOUT THE ART IN THIS BOOK

The artwork was created using pencil, ink, rubber stamps, halftone photographs, silkscreen, Zipatone, and Photoshop. Many of the textures and shapes used thoughout the book come from photographs I took while visiting Paris. Other photos' credits can be found with the copyright information at the front of the book.

WANTED!

APR 2 1 2016

WANTED!

ESSIONAL
MINAL!

WANTED!

PROFESSI
CRIMI